Other titles in the UWAP Poetry series (established 2016)

Phillip Hall is family to Blackfullas ... a champion who writes like truth ... he sees Country like me, like a lot of Blackfullas – seeing the minute, and seeing the inferences.

Paul Collis, winner of the 2016 David Unaipon Award

Phillip Hall, you loved our kids and worked very hard, always smiling and planning a camp. You respected Culture and listened. So we care for you very much. You are our friend and poetry mentor – thank you.

**Jeanette Yawanjibirna Charlie,
Yanyuwa Language Teacher**

Fume

Phillip Hall

Phillip began living in Borroloola in 2011 when he went to work there as a teacher of sport and camps. He does not identify as a First Australian though Nana Miller has adopted him into Gudanji family. Here he has shared the rich culture of the Wualiya Clan of the Karranjinni (Abner Ranges) who speak the Gudanji language. Phillip's nana gave him the skin name of Jabala. She also gave him the traditional or bush name of Gijindarraji; she wanted him to have this because it was the traditional name of her pop. Phillip's mother is the goanna and emu though Nana Adie always joked that his true Dreaming was the 'worry bird' (also known as the curlew). But the town of Borroloola is also home to the people of the Yanyuwa, Marra and Garrwa language groups. Phillip feels very fortunate to call these people friend and family.

In 2012 Phillip established Diwurruwurru (The Borroloola Poetry Club). Diwurruwurru means message stick and is used by permission of the Traditional Owners. Diwurruwurru has collaborated with Lionel Fogarty, Amanda King, The Australian Literacy and Numeracy Foundation, Blank Rune Press and the Northern Territory Writers' Centre to perform at festivals & to create a film and chapbook of their work – a wonderful celebration of creativity in the Gulf.

Phillip now lives in Melbourne's Sunshine where he is a very passionate member of the Western Bulldogs Football Club. He loves to cheer, and to honour the First Australians of the Northern Territory's Gulf of Carpentaria.

Phillip Hall
Fume

Poetry

First published in 2017 by
UWA Publishing
Crawley, Western Australia 6009
www.uwap.uwa.edu.au

UWAP is an imprint of UWA Publishing
a division of The University of Western Australia

A catalogue record for this
book is available from the
National Library of Australia

Designed by Becky Chilcott, Chil3
Typeset in Lyon Text by Lasertype
Printed by McPherson's Printing Group

This project has been assisted by the Australian
Government through the Australia Council, its arts
funding and advisory body.

 uwapublishing

Singing with the

Yanyuwa, Marra, Gudanji & Garrwa

of

Borroloola,

in the Northern Territory's

Gulf of Carpentaria

And in loving memory of
Nana Miller (nee Raggett):
proud Custodian of Gudanji Culture,
Traditional Owner of McArthur River Station,
Jungkayi for Jayipa (Catfish Hole),
my teacher –
there is so much Sorry Business

Contents

Acknowledgement of Country

Carpentaria Running the Flag

Heat radiates off the back-broken
bullish escarpment where lost cities rise
as columns of silica crusted in iron
above pocketed zinc seams, gouged cattle plains
and salt flats; a backcountry driven bony
even as floods flush north to the Gulf
and I cast bait, slipping past crocs and luring barra
on bloodied lines; channelled, shimmering,
verdant as those caught thrash
on sand before being parcelled in paperbark
and sweetened in coals amidst bunched
golden beard grasses and cathedral mounds; the Savannah Way
a graded fence line vanishing into the rusted
landscape where a charged sphere percolates

Indigenous space.

Bad Debt

As a child I lived in the Blue Mountains of NSW. My house stood a stone's throw from the Great Western Highway and railway line: noise and bustle, the Indian Pacific, Mack trucks. From our front veranda I gazed up that highway, west, all the way to Perth, while outside our back fence was a gully. I mucked up, the artful dodger escaping jobs, turning to outside-the-back-gate.

Once in my gully, I was an adventurer or an explorer, maybe even an escaped convict. One daydream, however, bound itself to my child imagination more than any other: I was a lost Aboriginal, defiant, living in Eden. As a child, I hero-worshipped this ideal, with almost no sense of the cruel barbs of colonialism's crooked paths, even though my best friends were three Aboriginal boys – Kimberly, Michael, Peter – adopted by a local family. We went to the same school, Blaxland Primary, and together we got up to such joyous mischief.

At the head of our gully was a series of small rock pools surrounded by thick native bush and blackberry and filled with tadpoles, insect larvae and dragonflies. From the rock pools, the creek flowed a few hundred metres before reaching a small waterfall. At the base of this sandstone cliff line there was a cave hidden in the shady bottom of the gully. Here we kept a tarp, billy, matches and a knife. With this knife we were blood brothers, and while we never got permission to stay in our cave overnight, from it such bravery was planned.

If you struggled down the creek line for about an hour, over slippery and mossy rocks, you came to the Glenbrook Gorge. Here there was much more water: fish and yabbies, sometimes turtles. Big boys told stories of how the trees around these swimming holes were filled with snakes. Snakes so big that they swung from tree to tree and from one side of the gully to the other. But the truth is that in all the time we spent down there, snakes were a rare spotting: a death adder, a diamond python, a few red-bellied black snakes, that was all. We once saw a wallaby, sometimes echidnas and lyrebirds, lots of blue-tongues, water dragons and kookaburras. The bush was a marginalised place, squashed by suburbia and kept in our child minds, just for us. We traced moss, lichens and fungus with our fingers, carved sandstone, threw rocks, made spears and ochre and sucked the honey from Mountain Devils.

Looking back on those childhood ramblings, I might wish that our joy had been more lasting; that play could somehow find a path through the thicket of race, but of course colonial colours are indelible. As an adult I continue to play in the bush, to remember my friends, but teasing out a just path where they have the same advantages as me has been a burden of lament.

As an adult I have been able to make the bush the place of my professional life. I work as an outdoor educator, taking small groups of predominantly teenage participants into remote national parks for up to a fortnight. All of my expeditions are intended to foster respect for First Australians and are based on a model of minimum-environmental-impact bushwalking in difficult and trackless terrain. I reject the idea of 'wilderness', as racism – yet another version of *terra nullius* – and challenge those with whom I walk to cherish the custodianship of First Australians. The following extract from my poem, 'Learning on the Line', attempts to encapsulate my approach to this type of experiential learning:

> At last the end of Narrow Neck
> and we climb the cliff line, down
> to Medlow Gap and two hours more
> to the Mob's Swamp cave, our camp.
> *What bastard promised this would be our 'easy' day?*
> With sugar levels low, the careless
> push for camp fractures certain tempers
> so amidst some cranky laughter I readdress the rules,
> motivating our final effort when freed of packs,
> a coffee and a freeze-dried meal will make
> the relief of conversation around

the fire at night, before the luxury
of an overhang's dirt floor,
the Milky Way and the full moon lighting
its veneer outside.

We wake at dawn, or thereabouts,
a cold fog in the casuarinas
outside. Breaking camp a little later
than I might have liked we look
at maps, measuring the angles
of our route and set to climb
Warrigal Gap; contouring round
the western edge of Merrimerrigal
we traverse Mt Dingo to the Bushwalkers'
War Memorial – Splendour Rock.
Lunching with views of the days
ahead – the Cox's Gorge, the Gangerang Ranges
to Kanangra Walls – a grasstree – *Xanthorrhoea australis* –
high on conglomerate rock collects
our attention like regimental colours
and provokes Smithy: *Come off it Phil, it's a blackboy,*
a spear throwing blackfella, quick, let's souvenir the shaft.
I sweet-talk the group with the adventure
of bush tucker and craft, a one plant supermarket:
spears, fire sticks, sugar, grubs and glue –
You think this is wilderness. It's 'Country'.

This is my idealistic approach with the kids I lead on hike: to deflect
racism with humour and to challenge with knowledge and respect.

In 2011 I was offered the opportunity of a lifetime to work in
remote Indigenous education. There was a position vacant for a
sport and camp teacher at Borroloola, in the Northern Territory's
Gulf of Carpentaria. Borroloola is now located on Yanyuwa country.
But after close to 150 years of massacre and dispossession the town
is also shared with members of the Garrwa, Marra and Gudanji
peoples. Borroloola's Indigenous people have been forced to hold

much of their shocking frontier contact history locked away inside of themselves. The Gulf was northern Australia's thoroughfare for the cattle industry from very early on in the colonial period, trafficking cattle from northern Queensland into the Territory and Kimberley. The Gulf was once home to at least twelve Indigenous language groups; four remain. A map of the Gulf includes such place names as 'Massacre Hill' and 'Skull Creek'. The old people in Borrolooola, the bardibardi and malbu, were grown up on eyewitness accounts of massacres. They remember stories of those poor old fullas, like thieves, collecting the bones for remembrance in caves. I have wept at these 'strong places' with Gudanji family. The trauma, like seismic tremors, repressed still.

This anger and loss is locked inside Borroloola's First Australians, who make up around 95% of the town. Borroloola's population is around 600-700 in the Dry Season, when the town is already hopelessly over-crowded in poorly maintained and inadequate housing. But during August's rodeo week, and in the Wet Season, this population swells to 1000-1200 as more and more people are schooled into town by rodeo fever and flooding waterways. Over-crowded and poorly maintained housing is the cause of so many health problems: sleep deprivation, scabies, boils, head lice and a plethora of stress-related illnesses. The flag is raised every day: black for the people the country sings; yellow for the sun percolating with energy and life; red for the country rich with iron and rusted in blood.

It is said that only 'missionaries, mercenaries and misfits' move to the Territory. I am a missionary and misfit. I believe in education, proselytising the downtrodden, and self-sacrifice. I want to empower Indigenous youth to make their own choices, to thrive in liberal democracy, and to assert their own choices and culture. But when I moved to Borroloola I wanted to do too much, too quickly, and I rubbed myself out in earnestly trying to create programs and opportunities that most Australians would assume as their right. This sounds very 'Whitlam-esque' and, of course, I crashed in punitive and bullying systems concerned, it seemed to me, with conformity, collecting statistics and doing the least amount of work. My 'good fight' now includes a slippery dependence on alcohol (so common in the Territory), self-harm and severe depression (including an attempt to take my own life). My air-evacuation out of Borroloola to Darwin Hospital and then on to Cowdy (a psychiatric ward) was the subject of government investigation in 2015. It found that I had been the victim of a workplace injury, and that the most convenient outcome was to compensate me at the expense of silence. I am still not at liberty to disclose the details of my settlement with the department or the findings of the investigation into my breakdown. It is the intervention that I required in late 2014. I returned to Borroloola – I am family – but I have found living amongst so much remote and repressed trauma a dangerous thing.

In Borroloola I worked as a teacher of sport and health programs, and after school I coached AFL with the goal of taking teams away to participate in carnivals. These opportunities were offered to the kids as part of a wider incentive program to encourage school attendance and good behavior. Participation required me to not only coach and manage the team but also to drive a coaster bus to and from the event (a minimum round trip of 1500 kilometres). My job was to reengage disadvantaged Indigenous kids by developing these sport and camp opportunities designed to teach emotional resiliency, cooperative group learning, safe decision-making and environmental education. And I worked with all the self-destructive passion of a zealot.

Teaching in a place like Borroloola is very stressful – even when your work mainly involves the coaching of sport. Over-crowded and poorly maintained housing leads to many health crises as I have outlined. Sleep deprivation, and dehydration from not drinking enough water while living in such hot and humid conditions, causes much irritability (especially during the difficult afternoons). These conditions, which are even further complicated by issues around payback and family responsibility, create the atmosphere for a lot of conflict and fighting. And this challenging behavior is very stressful for a non-Indigenous teacher to manage. Fortunately for remote schools in the Northern Territory, there is a commitment to employing local First Australians as home-liaison officers and as teaching assistants, to sort through these complicated yet important cultural issues. During my time in Borroloola I worked alongside many glorious First Australians who fulfilled these roles. And one of these was a Gudanji elder named Lady Miller who would become one of the most important people in my life. Tragically this elder passed away in 2016 and is now known as Lady Miller or Nana Miller.

Nana Miller had an enormous capacity for love and goodwill. But more than this, she somehow exuded a quiet, proud strength that brought you into her orbit. She challenged you to want the best for these Borroloola kids but also to embrace enough humility to accept that not all complications were easily navigable (unfortunately I really struggled to accept enough of this humility). By early 2013, I had already been in Borroloola working hard for a couple of years, nurturing strong relationships, when one day outside the staffroom, there was a secondary male student running amok and stoning the school buildings. The school immediately went into lockdown, a not unusual routine as we reacted from one crisis to another.

After D.R.'s frustrations and rage had subsided I found myself outside with him attempting to pacify his remorse and shame. D.R. had poor hearing, and limited capacity to communicate orally, though he was a gifted athlete and proud Gudanji man. His difficulties in communicating meant that he was often unable to control his temper when confronted with injustice or setback. But I had bonded with him very closely. He was one of the first students to welcome me to Borroloola, and he never failed to growl at any fellow student who he considered was acting disrespectfully towards me. D.R. was in my secondary boys AFL team, and so we spent many hours together on the field, in the gym and running up sand dunes. On this occasion he felt that he had been treated unfairly by being excluded from a vocational education opportunity to gain a certificate in quad bike riding. It was an experience that he had been looking forward to for a long time. I was an old whitefulla, usually found lifting weights in a gym or boxing a punching bag, but here I was weeping with D.R. - crushed by yet another collapse in goodwill.

I think it was this episode with D.R. that finally made up Nana Miller's mind to 'formally' adopt me into her family and Gudanji Culture. One weekend she drove me out to Jayipa (Catfish Hole) to meet family and Country. She discerned that she was my nana, or arwuju, and this meant that my skin name was Jabala. She also announced that my traditional or bush name would be Gijindarraji. She wanted me to have this because it had been the traditional name of her pop. And she sung me as jungkayi for Jayipa. This was one of the proudest days of my life and began a long journey of discovery and enculturation that often saw me out bush with Gudanji family on holidays and weekends. This new arrangement changed the nature of my relationships with the Borroloola community. For one thing I was now related to half the town. And due to the circular nature of skin relationships D.R. became my 'little dad' (or *lil-dad)*, a relationship that he never stopped grinning about.

In early 2012 my love affair with the Borroloola communities found another practical outlet. Knowing my interest and respect for Culture many of the kids with whom I worked, and their parents and grandparents, began to share stories and memories with me. This storytelling soon merged into meals and games around a campfire. Later I was asked if I would enjoy writing some of these stories down. This passion became the Borroloola Poetry Club and we started to meet every Friday after school (and sometimes out bush on weekends and school holidays). We were given permission to call our club Diwurruwurru (which means 'message stick' in Yanyuwa) and, despite all my hilarious poor attempts at spelling and pronouncing words in Aboriginal English and Language, we soon had enough written celebration to begin appearing at festivals and in publications. I will have a lot more to say about this First Australians storytelling group in my later essay, 'The Stick'. Diwurruwurru was always a lively creative place where family and friends would meet to explore, experiment and assert First Australians Culture and Story. The message stick that it generously shared was one of pride, respect and strength.

My first book, *sweetened in coals,* was launched at the 2014 WordStorm in Darwin, the festival of the Northern Territory Writers' Centre, with a busload of Diwurruwurru members present at the party. This book was the product of about twenty years of writing. I write slowly. And I was busy working and growing up my own family (as the glorious Olga Masters said: 'my best books'). Between

2011 and 2014 I was too busy with Diwurruwurru, and my work, to complete very much writing of my own. During this time I only wrote five of the poems that are to be found in *Fume:* 'Carpentaria Running the Flag', 'Borroloola Blue', 'Concourse', 'Borroloola Class' and 'Dystopian Empire'. The remaining thirty poems of *Fume,* were all written in Borroloola in 2015, after my breakdown and while I was recovering at home. It is important that they were all written on Country and while I was physically close to my Borroloola family and friends. The whole manuscript was reshaped over 2016–2017 in Melbourne's Sunshine where I now live. I write to honour the First Australians of the Northern Territory's Gulf of Carpentaria and to interrogate colonialism's twisted and violent paths. I also try to write myself back to health.

The five years that I lived at Borroloola were some of the proudest times of my life. My welcome into Gudanji family and Culture was such a generous acclamation of my work, the memory of it still brings me to tears. I cherish every moment out bush with family learning about Culture and bush tucker, our AFL tours, the annual excursions to the Tennant Creek Poetry Festival with the Australian Literacy & Numeracy Foundation, teaching the kids to play hockey and waterpolo (with competitions for trophies), and the raucous joy of Diwurruwurru. In Borroloola I gained so much, but it also came at a considerable cost, I just couldn't help breathing in trauma. I should have been more resilient, but I wasn't, and it made me sick. After my breakdown, when I could no longer do the work that I loved so much, I was filled with shame for a long time. I am still knotted with it (and with the scars of my self-harm). Am I returning to health? Can the Borroloola kids, whom I love so much, expect the same opportunities that I assumed as a boy running amok in the Blue Mountains bush?

Fume

Note Regarding Cultural Sensitivity

Many of the poems in *Fume* respond in a very intimate way to the barbs of colonialism's crooked paths. Permission, from First Nations people who own these stories, has been given for me to include my poems about them in *Fume*.

'Walk up Tank Hill': *Yalinga* is Indigenous language (Yanyuwa/ Garrwa) in the Gulf region of northern Australia for 'foreskin'. This word should not be voiced out loud as it is connected with Ceremony. It should be read as 'foreskin' during public readings. I have permission to write this word, as it is another example of generational/cultural crisis in a post-contact world. It is often spoken in the Gulf, usually by young males, to cause offence.

'Hand Back': on November 26, 2015, a native title determination by the Federal Court returned some rights of surviving Gudanji clans to hunt and hold ceremony at McArthur River Station. The contemporary accounts of the massacre of First Nations that occurred on this station, and which I quote from in this poem, can be found in Tony Roberts, *Frontier Justice: A History of the Gulf Country to 1900*, (Queensland University Press, St Lucia, 2005), pp 168-185. McArthur River Station managers and stockmen knew one of these massacres as the Malakoff Creek Massacre. They cynically named it so to celebrate one especially bloodstained Russian battlefield. This poem responds to the offensive values of those who carried out these massacres, and of those (all of us who are not First Australians) who benefit from the dispossession of First Nations today. Too much of our reparation is piecemeal and symbolic.

Walk up Tank Hill

For my lil-dad, Dwight Raggett, Gudanji man

I was Carpentarian born again
               and your eyes growled
                         give him a go:

      so a team sprinted
            in and out of drills, a left
and a right, a drop
           punt and the perfect hooting
           screamer. We ran on sand
      and cheered even as certain tempers fractured –
the *life style choices* of remote Indigenous
                             living:

      then one afternoon, after
all that dreaming on a white lined
           and dusty oval, with a swim in a pool,
      it was the foot-pad, a singles
track up Tank Hill:

           that stifling
climb, bare feet stone-hopping burnt,
      the dragons scuttling
           for their shade:

climbing
      in familial chatter, someone up line
      farted, and amidst howls
of *yalinga* and *black hole,*
      those poked 'I'll bash ya' eyes,

        a rock silenced
everyone, grazing
        my shoulder as it speared
            on past:

        a reshuffle
in some humour moved
            us on, picking
        berries as someone shared
a little law: *dis one bark medicine,*
                dat one tucka, not now but,
            he drop ta ground den
                millad mob eat'im, an d'rectly
            millad sugarbag'll sing:

it was all
        red-hot and heady
        as wilderness grew
into country and you were my map, amplifying
            a lore's perspective:

            soon we discovered
        the knoll's summit and it was broken
                gaze through scrub:

water
           pumped, slantwise, from bores
           to this hill top, a steel storage
tank burning silver in this late
                          afternoon heat:

       water banked
underground for millennia and tapped
           in manicured access holes sung
                  in law and now siphoned
for consumption under an authority's bill:

              we repossessed
and the Gulf lifted
           and opened to dark
stringybarks and woollybuts amongst spear
grasses and cathedral mounds – the centuries
           of law disrupted/defiant, singing
a storm still:

              so hard
to imagine a straight spine
but here they were, a raw ironstone,
           rusted but ochred dancing
                                  still
since dwelling off country is to wait for sickness
           like diwurruwurru lantana-
                  engrafted:

heat shimmering
with shadows on cave walls, the red hands
stencil-blown for company, a mark
signed on a canvas of their making, already
weathering back to wild stone:

you perched
in the elbow of a woollybut just
where my snapshot shows you, grinning straight
back at me:

so in the nature
of circular skin ties:

me a middle-aged munanga; you
my lil-dad, the teenaged ruckman shining
even as storms grazed
side-long with the ache of your sniffing,
a sadness-stone like the ngabaya's bony
choking clutch threatening dead-of-night torment
on top this country's Tank Hill.

Borroloola Blue

All around our steel home's broad bull-nosed veranda
we'd jack-hammered rock, dug garden beds and ponds,
fenced an oasis as we planned for shade, blossoms, wildlife and fruit.
Amongst the natives we'd cultivated

paw paws, frangipanis, mangoes, bananas ... Security
lights drew tree frogs and geckos; a Greek chorus
of bellowed crawks and clicking chick chacks;
an agile profusion alternating with contentment and strife.

But that season, in the build-up to the Wet,
it was the raucous rocket frogs' ratchet-like croakings
we noticed most. Each night the males made our ponds
throb with their rapid yapping calls, withdrawing at sunrise

when grass finches postured on the lips of ponds,
flicking their tails and singing a series
of squeezed rasping notes; white-gaped honeyeaters
threaded a path through foliage and blossom

as Papuan cuckoo-shrikes tore paw paws and mangoes.
Then one night, at the build-up's end, as we drank
chardonnay on ice, Yanyuwa youths ran amok
on ganja, throwing stones and chiacking at our padlocked gates.

It only ended when [sorry name] leapt on our fence,
screaming at stars, before lightly climbing
a power pole like a cabbage tree palm –
an unabashed athleticism electrified

in the fall.

Brolga Clan

For Noela Anderson, Alan Baker, Jeanette Charlie, Maria Pyro &
Patsy Shadforth:
Yanyuwa, Gudanji & Garrwa teachers
(who first orientated my Borroloola cheer)

From the town camps, junk
      is spoiling like a sniffed fume's squall
      and a clan of brolga are trumpeting
          their distaste, regally
bowing and high-stepping their preened mettlesome
          chests and arching their wings upwards
in a whoosh of grey-ochred law:

          from around the bend a four-wheeler spins
      like a shanghaied wedgie collapsing
to maggots on the ground:

the beloved Macassans' hoary old tamarind trees; their emerald
          exotic glass and steel
      tools paving the trepang and shell starlit highway
colonially rutted by uniformed rifle collared lines:

      behind us the old police station – a poor
      museum to frontier orders – cathedral
mounds rising out of spear grasses, ironwoods brandishing
          clumps of mistletoe – and their tiny
pastel chewing gum fruits – barbed wire fencing,
      a rodeo's rusty dust bowl, the prick-hard
              football ground:

      and from those sidelines I was stamped to cheer
barefoot cyclones, like a satellite stepping
              stars.

Concourse

For the Borroloola mob

In my troopie dodging dogs, ditches and broken bikes
I'm at a camp of concrete blocks,
                    crushed soft drink cans and verandas strewn
                                        with mattresses:

here each building's bound
                    to a street-front white-and-blue steel sign
            a corporatised prescription
'No Liquor, No Pornography'
                    and scratched 'munanga on you':

        hey jigga, Malbu leans in close
let's get dem young ones bush:

        our complement of kids forearmed
    their gear crammed in garbage bags
                        we take to the Crossing
                a bridge built to span
flooding waters and golden middens of XXXX cans;
        in these footings Malbu discerns disturbance
dat bridge wrong way, dis here Waralungku, Hill Kangaroo Dreamin',
                    an dem spirit fullas stir strife:

        but we're soon bumping along savannah plains
    past starkly skeletal eucalypts
                    and the diamond-tessellated trunks
    of cycads and pandanus with their crowns

of palm fronds; and Malbu waves me on
    paperbark's Brolga Dreamin',
        d'rectly millad river'll sing:

behind us the kids laugh animated
    stirring and teasing in-and-out of their seats
their hands and eyes and mouths
       a liquid warbling
only partly accessible to me
though I know they want the music changed
      as Malbu growls *you mob got worms or what?*
      get yous black bunyis sittin' an soft down
   this blackfulla William Barton's didjin'
      yous show some respect now:

      look here mista! ... stop dat way! ...
the boys peering at the window are silenced
    as Malbu agrees *da twin trees ... might be somethin' ...*
      you know, big business ...
      dem old people watchin'
   dis one big kujika
  an he come kickin' against the pricks all through here
so with our kids behind me tracing
    their fingers on my whitefulla skin
and Malbu's arm round my shoulder I lean
      into country; a pair of slender
   messmate trees with darkly scarred
   trunks – a daredevil didj's drumfire:

rounding a bend in the gravel road
　　　　　　　the kids are chiacking and hooting *camp!*
Malbu allocates jobs, I recce an abseil site
　　　　　pondering my eco spiel as they cut down
a three-metre cyprus pine *no mista, he burn bright*
　　　　　　　　　　　　smoke dem mozzie too ...
　　　　an soon you dig taddle with us mob
in'im dry swamp ... Malbu assures me
　　　　　jigga, dis bush tucker make millad blackfulla mob shiny
　　　　　　　　an strong but do it proper law way
　　　　　　　　　everythin' in da song:

　　　　later downstream from cast nets and hand lines
I'm watching flows at the rivers' confluence
　　　　　– a red and brown twin load, swirling, suspended –
　　　　　look here mista, twobula runnin' one:

　　　　true god, we really are an arterial kaleidoscope
　　　　of silt-laden language.

Borroloola Class

For Noela Anderson

You open early, wooing
 them with air-conditioned
 promise in the beginning of light
 and watching through glass
 saturated thermals resounding
 as a low rolling highway of cloud
 channelled from the Gulf and piped
 the horizon long, so amidst
 the closed in busy teasing and pranks
 you challenge and distract gathering
 rapport as nana growls: *hey you mob*
 listen now an show mista dat cloud
 so as the class calms, Blaze gets crackin':
 millad mob know dat Julayarriyarri
 an he bring rain an all dem bats an birds
 dem old people did tell us dat, poor fullas,
 an if you come modaka out bush wid millad mob
 us dance dat storm like kardu buckin' bullocky –

a screwed-up muscle-sprung bellowed barrel
 like a didged rodeo's cheerin' mental-as-anything king.

Millad Mob da Best!

(with Diwurruwurru)

for Patsy Shadforth & Borroloola's kids

we likem dat Borroloola Rodeo
my kardu im gotta ridem dat big one bullocky
dat bull im jump really really high
im buck too much, makem dirt thunderin dust-burst
an big mob snot grunt from im nose
an dat bullocky im got wide open bash ya eyes
an im body like bullet train growlin dat mad one crowd
so kardu he hang on very very tight for millad mob
an e bin win dat big one trophy
makem all so proud a hallelujah
saviour one of all dem deadly dagger rides

*

*

wen do gate crack open my big one buja come crashin
out on gun fired screwed-up muscle ngabaya of a horse
come on buja, hang on
dat big one horse, e bin bash, buck an sling
wid so much hate an really really high
buja bin hold on cowboy roped on tight
dat horse e bin make biggest mob blackfulla roar
like baribari burst but buja bin ride on an on an on
e bin win big pack money an millad mob all so teary proud

*

*

we bin get up an hab-im gooda one feed
us mob so excited rowdy
no one bare foot on tis shiny one best of day
us mob all cowboy boot, bull hide hat, silky showoff shirt,
trouser an chaps wid mad one colour of fringe an fray
we bin jumin da mudika
an we bin go race rodeo ground
mimi an kukudi bin come too
an dey bin singin us mob bullocky dreamin song
dey bin learnin us mob
for to sing im an everyone deadly safe
we like learn for singin us mob song
for ceremony, culture, land an law
millad mob strong in dat rodeo an in dreamin us proud

*

Icy-pole Trade

We are again exchanging
our tokens as the Gudanji mob tease
with their sanitized
Ariel performances of mermaids
who lay on rocks with their golden flowing
ease, waiting for some rustling, a quiver
on the wind when...
                    the story shifts
again: *let's swap*
a 'mermaid' for the old ones' 'nuwalinya',
your 'girl' for their 'munga-munga' and the veil
is rent (*tru god*) to the Carpentarian
transformation of windmills and bores
into white-ochred munga-munga who smear
purplish-white puffball plants
on their thighs, forming and naming country
in a torrent, journeying on...
                    for the cheeky
these nuwalinya are appalling
when wild: ripping arms and cracking
ribs in a white water's ruptured
rolling drowning...
                    I'm in a wormhole – receiving
in tongues – but *you right mista,*
dey bin lovely when dey grow quiet an who knows
an inside-out coconut might sweeten in dat lovin'-up

                              drownin'...

Lullaby

Cradled in our family lounge, the blood
spurted in time with my heart's beat,
from my right buttock's gash as everyone
slept. Too ashamed at the dark-calling
to cry for help or sleep, I leaked
into shock. Damp death dragged
me from childhood. And I sleepwalked
my nightmare onto rooftop to jump
the dark – a fence-line's black
steel star-picket my landing ground. For months after
mum hung tins from every
door and window to keep
me in and dark's drag out. A tear splitting
blood-soaked tangle saved in dawn's muddle
when the scar and adult fear of balconied
apartments failed to out-grow afterbirth's rattle.

*

*

But now you, my Gudanji kin, are weeping
your cruelest, purest fear. The children hounded
at night by scraping nails, a window pressed bedraggled
burnt face, a bony clutching
reach. One night 'M' peered too long, and with everyone
asleep, the ngabaya sleepwalked him outside, to climb
cottage roof, and pressing him into the noose, his jump
brought a bone breaking jolt
to arm and leg, a rope-burned
throat, the terror crouching, as night-time panic
fled to Borroloola's clinic, alarm,
and morning after air-evacuation to Darwin –
a horror chased brooding that only children
see, adults forever dodging
ahead, a sibylic familial scent to unbolt
the scream in your ear like a baribari –
the moon-eyed, screwed-up shooting flash
of it, the drop, and the forever branded brawl.

*

Inheritance

Bigger than Christmas,
the Borroloola Rodeo announces
       itself with a mushrooming of camps
       as show trucks and outstations
chorus below a starlit big dipper
out on the edges of town:

       I unroll my swag
with Buffalos – the Gudanji mob
       from Bauhinia Downs, Cow Lagoon
       and Devil Springs – where this year's mood
is a carousel cracker in acclaim:

at the camp centre
       a 55-gallon drum is suspended
       between the forks of two trees
          by ropes bound
       to their anchor points
       with the neatest of figure-eights;
a mastery of makeshift mechanical bull:

       out on the edges
the kids practice their hondas,
       an overhand knot with a stopper
       at the end threaded through
and tightened down
       to form a nearly-perfect halo,
the lasso is a dream flung
              bang-on:

throughout our camp
tarpaulins hover like magic carpets
         giving shade and privacy
as ropes and uprights are fastened
                   with rolling hitches –
      a season's banked domestic security:

and this year our ropes lash
               together such calm relief
         in the managed risk of a rodeo's spills:

      this year we are spared
the dawn drop and swing
when the rope is laid down
                   in a wide sideways 'S',
         the end wrapped round thirteen
times to form a loop tightened
for the end:

this year
      when dawn breaks
the bull rider's eight second rattle
               is our only breathless

                         yield.

Dawn Song

For gangu, William Miller
& the Gudanji Devil Springs community

I strode through bush in the Gulf's full-moon half-dark.
Somnambulant air, an ambush predator's stillness,

not a bullocky, not a brumby, but all thirsty
and cast in fear. From our campsite I followed a dry

creek where my footprints faltered
on fractured iron, eroded rusted

rubble, piled to the ridge lines that I perceived
as a pair of conjoint arcs, an earth artist's

reflexive refuse. And looking away I saw the Gudanji's Devil-
Devil Dreaming: megalithic in grievous grey, a breakaway

exile, a slyboots bereft of his ancestor-wife.
I passed by this iron-capped mesa with those vehemently

remembered howls of a ngabaya's clutching choking reach. Grey
ghostly fragments of an ashen lore-fed world.

I shuddered in starkness above scarps and knick points.
The worry-bird's drawn out wailing *weeer-eearr* turned

and it was dawn. The wind picking up, leaves
rustling and ashes blowing

across the ground, familial chatter, turtles cooking
and gangu cupping his hands in percussion and quietly singing,

lifting his country: making it good, making it listen.

Waterlily Light Well

The Wet Season's first rain
is a buckjumper's cock-a-hoop eight-second rattle
                    flushing free
Barrawulla's space in white plumage and upswept sulphur crest
            as pent-up raucous screech blooms
        spear grasses and the thrown elongated green hues
        casting to salmon-pink and deepening rust-coloured streaks:

                bats and more birds return from the north
        riding fat highways
        of morning glory clouds
                as thick life again floods
from Karranjinni's limestone cliff-cradled
        swamps and billabongs:

and every afternoon there's abundance
        in the sky percolating
                this ancient seabed
                of squeezed silica blocks
raised as vertical fractures and gouged
                into chasms and pancaked towers – the stacked
havens of rock figs, grevilleas and palms – as Barrawulla sharpens
            his powerfully curved bill on his *lost cities* home,
            his mandibles articulated for crushing and tearing
a landscape's hunted wood-boring grubs:

Jagududgu's flightless sprawling
odyssey arrives in loose grey-brown and black quilled
law, highbrowing bright blue to bestow
on Barrawulla's billabong
sweet waterlily for song:

in this preened and chiseled country
the Yanyuwa and Gudanji bind in spirit form:
one a turbulently swept red coastal silt,
the other a limestone's cradled gold alluvium.
This confluence of ochre-enriched law
is pooled in Barrawulla's bedrock when evaporation
draws iron to surface –
the inside-story's business backbone of this place.

Mermaid Growl

Through the sweltering savannah we amble
between shade trees and honeycombed escarpment
    where a faint quiver of thermal plumes
        is a shape glimpsed riding high
above the rot and vapour of this world:

where an ancient sea bed is upheaved
    and fractured into stratified
blocks, eroding as columns, and conceived
    in this glare as akin
to Angkor's crumbling temple towers, a complex
    lost to rock figs and palms in oppressive
dregs of time:

    but to nana *this strong one country*
is pregnant with Barrawulla whose after-birth
        is a white and sulphur-crested mineral bleaching
    and the organ pipe formations
are Barrawulla's ravenous gouging
    of a fat country extracting
Gudanji boring grub remembering:

so at the edges of these crystal clear thermal springs
    there are cruel curling foams
and from underwater ledges and crevasses
        long trailing algae blooms
seem on the cusp of some metamorphosis
    like the larval-nymph dragonfly
in a long past volcanic age:

but nana reassures me: *it safe to swim, go on.*
Nuwalinya are quiet in this place
Bing Bong long way, they grow wild there
with them cheeky fishers
an that port dredgin' devastation:

and so I enter the warm mineral-rich waters
where elsewhere ensnarement trails
silver hair.

The Gudanji's Dry Stone Country

that skirmishing small man peewee paces
                    his country, stamping
         his *tee-hee* to his consort's echoing *pee-o-wee;*
         guarding his water coolamon of fermented
pounded pandanus laced with sugarbag:
         that poor old bugger tree frog reverberates
            like a washed-up storm-water pipe
but peewee's dashing dark bill pricks
         that dried up amphibian along
              - north   south   east   west -
until exhausted, close to death, that frog stones
         the coolamon gushing
         open all the sweet
shared streaming waters of a land:
         that peewee's payback
                to bash
           his own poor self releasing
        a streamy black-on-white dried up
           blood as frog teasingly
                        redoubles the wet

Gudanji Old Moon Curlew

a sliver of crescent-shaped light
amidst all dark matter
new moon new moon
digging the roots of waitawhile
– jikarri –
millad mob wash an crush an boil ta bogie
tis good healin' culture
poor old bugger curlew chick finish
and moon foretells darkness before resurrection
but curlew sticks to wild haunting
a sneaky wailing after bush babies
ratted by the gossipy full moon

Turtle Camp

*For my Yanyuwa friends
and two-way learning*

On classroom walls we paste
        this learning, monitoring
                life cycles and health,
in advertisement of eco-calling:

we sit under mango trees, interviewing
        family – Yanyuwa bardibardi
an li-Anthawirriyarra Sea Rangers – Maabayny
                is Sea Turtle Dreaming, pursued
        in the tracks of a turtle's hauled flight,
and a glaring crystal luminescence
                is gasped as air humid and heavy with salt:

each night we will sing
        this turtle and hatchling tide – measuring,
        tagging, collecting – in a surge
of sustainably flowing law:

        the bardibardi conspire,
and recruit me to collect more kids, to press
        on disinterested funding reengagement's claim
        where self-sabotage grinds
the canvas of those already beaten
                                low:

camp morning and the chick chacks
        flicker from bardibardi to me, while high
on worth I audition the 'what ifs'
        of environmental and medical risks
before the Bing Bong bus to the sea:

a mine's bullying 'no entry' soon disturbs
        a sickness site
        and iron ore dust suffocates
containment lines
                and we are silenced:

we bend round past this port
        for a dirt track where the Sea Rangers wait
like popeyes
                to ferry us to Carpentaria's heart:

                and soon we're motoring along
        the glass calm waters of the Gulf, dodging
reefs and sand bars with dolphins shooting
                        through our wake:

Yanyuwa rangers nostalgically
point to ancient Macassan camps and to ghosts
        of dugout canoes while bardibardi whisper
        into winds: *us all forgotten*
                lil-bit, millad mob who come behind...

on arrival we hoot
up the beach and pitch
our swags under stands of casuarinas
and I again give my eco-spiel about rubbish
                    plastic ingestion:

waiting for a night's
            science monitoring, I high-wire walk
my team-building initiatives and sports
            over a wet tropical paradise that has teeth –
reigning in exuberance to maintain
                                us whole:

when the tide turns
            we fish off a rocky point, casting
                        for bait before the jerk
of coral trout and parrot fish; knifing
oyster off the rocks; the kids know law, cooking
our feast in a ground oven where it is killed:

and later, from out of the night's churn
            and frothing sea-foam, a pregnant
                        hauled awkwardness back-handing
dry weight in a nest of sand
and thick clear mucus – a soft-shelled
                                leathery hoard:

with our field work complete the last turtle turns
     and the bardibardi chant, swaying
to the animal's rhythm
as the kids take small dancing steps, their hands raised
     waist high, palms upward, urging
the laboring turtle on –
     bawuji barra...
wingkayarra wingkayarra kayikaji ka-wingkala barra...
     yuwu wakara nyinku na-alanji wurrbi...

Build-up

The bardibardi call time
on mununga slogans of 'stop the boats';
        shaping-up and giggling
        their Macassan memories
of brown bodies coming ashore in a spray of surging sea:

for centuries these boat people cultivated
        tamarind trees in a highlight
                of northern fruits spoilt
                in another latecomer's scorched earth:

so, with the bardibardi, we integrated
        secondary programs: mapping
Macassan heritage sites and Australian detention centres,
        writing petitions and emails, researching
                and tabulating the figures
on massacres and stolen land, resistance,
                Eddie Mabo and 'Land Rights Now':

        we camped at Jawuma and Lhuka
where once the conch shell heralded
        Yanyuwa welcome to traders hauling
                a well learned reverential eye:

        we hunted trepang, shark fin,
sandalwood, the shells of turtle and pearl;
        mounting a classroom exhibition –
                our pot of rainbow trade:

and at Waralungku Arts the bardibardi collected
an exhibition on all the Gulf's 'boat peoples',
  all those sweet fruits and liar fruits
    carried by people from far away:

so, at year end, we bundled
  into troopies, and through
  an avenue of tamarinds, headed
for Massacre Hill:

  here an idyllic creek flat
nestled an ancient fishing weir at the foot
  of a spur's sweeping runway, up
to thrumming silence,
that bluff of pelted fruit:

here the vertical stratifications
of bedrock cut through
    cheeky and rough.

Fallen

After Barcroft Boake's 'Where the Dead Men Lie'
some of whose 'Earth's loved sons'
certainly committed massacres of First Australians

And for Diwurruwurru who wanted a bush ballad

In caves of commemoration
      That's where the bones now lie.
On ngabaya blasted earth tessellations
      That's where the blood was let dry.
Out where cattle were bred free
From *natives*, in a barbed wire
Stock whipped polity
      Out where violence carries on.

Washed in the billabong's brown flow,
      Over where the slain now lie.
Where emu gifts waterlily so people grow
      That's where the slain now lie.
Constructing ground ovens and stonewall
Fireboxes, processing a commonwealth's
Measured, speared-sprawl
      Out where havoc is now strong.

For centuries exotic trade flourished
      Out where the slain would lie.
In these relations First Nations were nourished
      Out where the slain would soon lie.
The first boat people were heralded by conch-shell
As traders carrying tobacco, arak and metal
For trepang and shells of pearl and turtle
      Out where nourishment was sung.

In these wastes Britannia rails at failure
      So that's where the slain now lie.
In the wild times cattle struggled to prosper
      So that's where the slain now lie.
With the liberal use of powder and ball
Britannia dispatches after herding them all
Over cliffs, bones bearing grim evidence of the fall
      Out where the victors pervade.

The .577 calibre Snider is a *splendid civiliser*
      Out where the slain now lie.
Firing a massive mushrooming reminder
      Out where the slain now lie.
And the Martini-Henry's rapid rate of fire
Brings them to a standstill, a .45 calibre choir
Unleashing on the *obstinate* a thresher's ire
      Out where the mighty are gun barrel straight.

The lawless frontier made reprisal inevitable
      Out where the slain now lie.
And a bloodhound's payback is irrevocable
      Out where the slain now lie.
Rakuwurlma is the Gulf's resistance fighter
Shadowing troublesome ghosts, tracking tighter
The nulla nulla blaze of his own notorious fire
      Out where the rage smolders and glows.

In caves of commemoration
      That's where the bones are let lie.
All but rubbed out in civil predation
      Out where crystal memories lie.
Sung in milk quartz, trauma is milled
In corralled country that is disturbed,
Yet defiant and bull-necked still,
      Because that's where history lies.

Talking English

The Gulf's ancient tongues are hobbled
by inherited trauma, gene-crackers

sadistically scabrous and burgeoning
in the remembered fluency of wire-tipped

stockwhips and all those manhandled
civilisers of a splendid frontier's orders.

And though munanga were not to prosper
in these mirages of pasture and surface water,

where crocs and distance preyed in circles,
a momentum remained to infest

and disturb, to see barbed wire fencing
and scorched stations spread like gravel

where barefooted dancers once sung
a bounty pressed intimately in ochre

and law. And so sacred trees were cut
dead, bones gathered in caves and girls

stolen as *pilot* were hobble chained
as sex slaves in a waste land dragged

to heel by Martini-Henry carbines
that at this critical moment were talking

English.

Dystopian Empire

After Les Murray's, 'An Absolutely Ordinary Rainbow'
which celebrates a city held by one man's weeping;
fighting too often arrests Borroloola

Gossip spot-fires in Borroloola's Big Camp,
excitement incites the Gravel,
at Malandari, shopkeepers look up from their stocktaking
and the whitefulla foreskins forget their power:
dem people fightin'! twobula bardibardi ini dirt
an dem whitefullas can't stop'em...

The grey nomad traffic to King Ash is incensed
at the effrontery, claiming a flotilla
with the miners for gawking. And crowds keep streaming
from the catchments, this build-up's broken:
there's two old women fighting down there
and no one can obstruct them.

The close combatants are tearing hair and stomping
toes; bowed knee to knee like breaking kindling; gouging
and screaming as though into mirrors: *jirda! dat munga*
cartin' yarn at me ini! The fierceness
of their fighting has the crowd banked up, pointing

and impotent in the late afternoon burning,
a dehydrated alcoholic crankiness; and the riot squad
is back in Darwin, worn out with the fighting,
their vacancy unfilled like the punch line of rainbows.

Some will say, in the years to come, that the young
blackfullas lit up their ganja, or sniffed,
at the spectacle; the expectant mums pissed
as coconuts fermenting in sand:
but that soap-box's bent boss-eyed.

What do munanga know of salutarily singing country?
Of the numinous mischievously stirring strife
amongst already sabotaged custodians whose kujika's scorched?
Who will tearfully sing him, big business, with millad mob
in the dirt, pressing forwards, hoping for peace?

We have the song,
So we have the land

For Borroloola's DanceSite,
& the Indigenous Traditional Dance Project,
Marlene Karkadoo Timothy
& Lia Pa'apa'a

This fighting town is in remission
for tonight pride is torch lit by stars
as *DanceSite* shakes-a-leg and stomps
a country whole. Assembling on blankets
in a dusty football ground our goals
have been transformed into outdoor cinema
as Chooky Dancers raise a storm
with (Dr G.) and Blue King Brown.
And as the bardibardi and malbu make ready, collecting
players of clap sticks and didj, the dancers and kids
flicker excitedly between blankets, all painted
and dressed in their tribe's colours. Tonight
everything is sacred by degree and in Language
as purple Garrwa perform the Nanny Goat Dance
and everyone cracks it. The golden Gudanji bosses
of the Nuwalinya cycle sing next in descending scales
their metamorphic visions of white-ochred munga-munga
as mermaids dancing with plaited
wet bark and windmill blades as feathers – striding
in a loop from bore to bore; dancing
and singing across country still; and then there's hush
as Yanyuwa men fly in red and white ochre, anklets
of leaves, bi-plane headdresses and wings
as arms spread wide for strength
stomped through the pelvis to ground in remembrance
of war's search and rescue service. *When a spirit*
passes on, it returns to country. This is our inherited
fight, to sing the song back to our land.

From on a Cloud Looking Down

In memory of Ginger Riley Munduwalawala
who passed away in Borroloola's Marra Camp, September 1, 2002,
& for Waralungku (the Borroloola Art Centre),
which is still the 'boss of colour'

Out of sight and out of mind
Borroloola is a bloom
of asbestos and neglect even as the flag flies black
for the people, yellow for the sun percolating
life, and red for the rust-
rich country sodden
in blood:

Waralungku is a flow apart
from Papunya dots, the quiescent ochre
tones and sacred rarrk of Arnhem Land
or the bi-chrome planar maps of the Western Desert:

Waralungku is an acrylic boss, mixing
and layering beams of colour
on horizonless, flattened and canvas forms, where silhouetted
ancestral figures stride
through country studded
with cowboys, billy-goats and donkeys – here the rodeo's rattle
has dreaming:

at Waralungku, landscape is a grand
sweep of intimate
minutiae, where it has to be seen, it must
be bright:

here eroded mineral outcrops
are seen in horizontal bands
as rivers coil, drawn

to the shallow luminescence
of the Gulf, and bright blue
skies collapse
in a monsoonal deluge that redeem
fat highways, flooding
a stone parched country
with turtles, bara, bats and birds:

painting the lagoon or river bend
where your family is boss, where title is a grip
of creation knowledge, closed
to the outsider, this is the inherited
fight, to make graphic
the deeds of native-

born law.

Poppy's Pools

For, and with, my Gudanji lil-Kardu,
Peter Chungaloo, Devon Butcher
& Garth Mulholland

Come wid millad mob
an us show you we jungkayi
where a Rainbow splits a cavern's coolamon
squeezing up our hot water, bubblin'
over dis pandanus fringed land
a crystal clear bogey:

dem cheeky mununga
have it all knotted
up in leases
but dis our pocket,
an millad mob sing dis
                    in da old way:

an all dat lovely warmth spillin' wild
          from da ranges' gap
            is a lofty soak
like a fat rainbow fizzin'
                    in dis storm of life.

hand (pay) **back** (out)

For Nana Miller (nee Raggett),
Traditional Owner of McArthur River Station,
who took me to the river's native title ceremony
and asked me to write this poem

Claimed in 1883 as the largest station ever
        by 1900 whole tribes were decimated
          in *that big ride-round through the ranges:*

the mounted-police and stockmen had sport
                  with a lead brand,
          herding whole clans:

at the head of one calamitous
          gorge by the extreme
head of the station's watershed
      we dispensed some good medicine
counting more than fifty in the mob:

we crept on, feverishly awaiting the signal,
          taking up positions
          at every vantage point
while higher and higher rose the morning star;
                all sleeping peacefully on:

        then the pandemonium
rang out with a single shot
with the *blacks rushing to all points*
        only to be driven back with deadly fire:

one big buck rushed forward
          so I dropped him
                  in his tracks:

later I was astonished
to find, instead of a buck, a splendidly built
young lubra:

when the melee was over
we counted fifty-two dead and for mercy's sake
we dispatched the wounded:

twelve more we mustered
to a fearful, mangled
fall:

the skulls and bones
bearing grim evidence
of the awful slaughter
enacted there:

and today the Native Title crows sit, shadowed
over Massacre Hill, to settle
by an illusionist's humbugging
and *hey presto, justice now* – a shitfaced palimpsest
over their
bottom lines.

Welcome to McArthur River Mine

The savannah is opened
for business with trinkets as a ruptured
dreaming site leaches
metals, acid and salt. This is business
hand-shaken cheeky
and fast. So amidst the broken
kujika and fragments of law you sing
our presence still to this river bend
where the Abner Range gives gold
ochre for ceremony streamy
with blood and where quartzite outcrops
guard this riverbed's cleavage
to a rainbow's animated pent-up clout.
So it is to this hydro majestic
you lead; to this sweep
of skeletal river gums, sandalwood and weeping
paperbarks whose leaves are sweet steamed
balm. And while kids hunt in mud
for waterlily bulbs, turtles and mussels
you take a coolamon of soaking sliced yam
to grind and make into ti-tree wrapped cakes:
this good hot tucka to pick us up an sing
this strong one inside-story...
      Next morning in drizzle we drive
past the mine's locked boom-gates and hulk
of combustible waste – pyrite iron sulphide stacked
in a reactive rising dump and releasing
plumes of toxic burn. And concealed
from the road is the river's sacred

rainbow serpent gouged
in high grade zinc and leaking
a river's bioaccumulation of mercury and lead; a flowing
numinous landscape now watched over by broken
                                        poisoned song.

Royalty

For millad Gudanji Miller & Raggett mob

              I drove out bush with family
again to Jayipa
                   a catfish hole lined
        with paperbark and river gum
and those gleaming quartzite outcrops
           like a silver and zinc plinth encompassing
                        dark sheet water:

we hopped, stinging, across the baked
             earth, a tessellated black
soil with small sand drifts gathering
         to the decaying stone-boiled edges:

                   and while nana fired
a billy, weaving
            pandunus frond sieves
we all crashed, energised
                  in the brown water's warm wash:

        in the late afternoon
cool relief as pop arrived to dig
a bush-turkey ground-oven
        we all set to work:

                    the boys
           took a cast net and hand lines
                         for barra
   while the girls hunted
                    in water, feeling
              in the mud
   for waterlily bulbs, onions and yams:

   later they tap-danced the mud
              sweetening our outlook –
                         a seismic detection service reading
              for hibernating turtles –
   a shelled familial finery:

              at nightfall
   our guts tight
   with their fill we fired
                    the billy and traced
              stars as pop smoked us
   in quandong, picking us up:

              and nana sang country, rousing
                         the scrub
   and a rainbow's payback on this mine's seepage,
   and another's foreshadowed hole in our burial grounds,
              mucking us up
              making us sick.

Shimmering Snake Slide

Having made me mugkbali you instructed
    me in the contours, the soaks and bluffs,
        of culture and law. You introduced
    me to country, to family
Sharing and humbugging. I was simply
    honoured to listen, to repeat
        after you the nuggets
    shared. You a stickler for
Accuracy and demarcating
    who was boss and speaker
        for what. You were a strong line
    of ochre, and the busier and
Closer I got, the deeper
    trauma sliced
        through on my thighs. You named me
    after your pop who growled once
Munanga were cartin' yarn and sharp
    with no respect. They scoured
        the country with axes and chains
    before lured to a caroled
Lagoon strong with a sleeping
    snake, these munanga saw
        that rainbow rear and spit
    air pressure to cyclonic low; a tsunami of
Lightning embittered discharge clearing
    space and impressing a rainbow's
        return. At a nearby oxbow, you sung
    those bonds to corroborate me

Jungkayi. I was assimilated,
        but one fisher-bigot was fast
                where he had no business and watched,
        going mad, the dead-of-night's white bolt rise –
The storm's combustion
        of all around. Law is always
                this shimmering slantwise slide.

Message Stick

A signed album of all our trips has me leapfrogging
every which way. This ledger of screamers
and goals by teenaged cyclones forever sprung

to bounce and step, flying elusively as zip-zip men
to the drop-punt and ready snap for goal. For a hooting
moment we bond in a combination of attack, learning again

how sweet friendship is and bouncing back
after the slung-to-ground tumult of being scored
against. The praise of family stops us,

and for a moment even the MCG can't contain our hearts,
as we floodlight this fluttering field. The album
simply called 'millad mob coach' is not only the path

pounded in the tangle and turmoil of the field: it is memory
of unwinding in hot springs, of camping in swags, camp fires,
of riding an escalator and lift to Darwin Waterfront dining.

For me it also celebrates the details of those who ride
up front: our bounced banter in a coaster bus, sharing
superstitions for crossing cattle grids and site stories

of Country: the lil-hairy man as glimpsed
shape – choking and cracking the disrespectful
dancer after dark; the mermaid – as a faint quiver in sparkling

water, trailing a filmy strangling clutch like algae bloom, a strainer's
ambush along a crevice's cruel crawling foam; and the long
Dreaming Trails of the ngabaya, emu and frog who journeyed

long way from Lajamanu into Queensland where emu is still sung,
but ngabaya and frog broke with sorry hearts, so this squatting rock
is Frog Dreaming, face full for Lajamanu, and Ngabaya Dreaming

is a tor on Vanderlin Island peering through the Gulf and now set
in such treasured tokens kept within an album's sleeves –
diwurruwurru as performance review delivered

to me in Royal Darwin Hospital's psychiatric unit.

Discharge

Charged up like the family tree swilling
with FASD I was a christ doll
crossing unsuitable
margins, a perfect
fool for trauma's inhalation
where intervention
obliged blood weeping, a gravity swelled
in remote miniature
with executive hounding
a cruel rip of whitewash tumbling
dreams:

craving worth I believed
my trade was sport
and camps to reengage and disrupt
through reward, but a partnership
of mine trust and office-bound leaders wanted
another cheeky dog:

prejudiced, I wanted
much from vocation, transgressing
boundaries, rubbing
myself out:

so when air evacuation requisitioned
I went valium-quietly
into the single-engine
straight-jacketed cabin, sailing roughly
into the tropical supercell's spawned
black anvil.

Fizzer

Outside a locked hospital room, I'm standing
in one more line to hand in my phone
for charging; here everything's auditioned
for agency in self-harming and bodily fluids
are taken away quietly – substances and stains
on a liver are the more verifiable of props –
but of all the necessary indignities, the night's
flashlight every two hours and hand-over
to *approved* gate leave chaperones
is pretty easy to accommodate.
During the day I eat to schedule, avoid
craft therapy, work
in the gym and sit around waiting
for a calling. This is trauma's unpicking
and the scratching just eggs
me on: *too many young ones passing away*
by suicide, the bashing
on grog an ice an sniffing, the boils
needing lancing, the stresses of shit-box
never enough housing, the racist barbs
and indifference of too many remote
incentive miscarriages. It's all ambush-
hinged me undone. And the more I fess-up
the more twisted the labyrinth: *yes, I drink to cut*
and use kujaka's phone to Jesus but
(and now I'm pleading) *don't drop*
me, (with some rueful irony) *I still mark and crash*

the ruck and even on one wobbly
knee, my kick's quite true. But as the docs
take notes I'm pretty sure what

they're prescribing.

Professional Conduct

After Jan Senbergs, 'Otway Night'

With all the swagger of Buckley's and none I bark
my soprano cacophony, like a howling
jackass, anchoring
a calling to be needed, to toss
zeal like a king tide
on rocks. On my left a sweeping
river bend through Devil-Devil Dreaming
where an ancestor trickster capitulates
to sorry-business and separation, a gleaming
outcrop of quartzite eroding to rubble
with baked earthen cracks creeping
to small drifts of sand. On my right
white-barked eucalypts stand
starkly skeletal before the dark
diamond-tessellated trunks of palms,
their crowns of fronds crowding
the lagoon, a big place pregnant
with the genesis of life. From my animal skin
hat a densely claustrophobic scavenger
wailing the land into being
and fastening a corroboree dance pose
to earth: ochre body paint, leafy dance anklets
and loin cloth. On my chest I emblazon
the racists' taunting
as a king plate, executive bullying
manifest in self-harm, reducing me to a ratbag's
dreaming avatar

– part man/part bush/part bird –
a precarious evocation of night's
load when grog will give license

and release.

mercenaries, missionaries, misfits

for Borroloola's whitefullas

from this knoll we measure
our starting lines
before descending
via a myriad of spurs and gullies, all those false starts
and retraced steps, emerging
like oil and water –
some seeking in the east a jeweled nadir,
a morning star tracking metamorphosis;
others a western dimness, deemed by some, the end of all their days

Cactus

That first night, released, in the Eco House
– bird song and wind leafing through canopy –
in the tree top room at Darwin's
George Brown Botanical Gardens
with the megapods scratch-tumbling the rot.

I stood at the screened black-louvered windows
and beneath me two orange-footed scrubfowls
scraped and poked through the humus
like cacti. Hungry composters, flight ready, and willing
me gone; their work bore fruit

though no conscious movement directed
their effort. They drilled in for grubs
and bugs as they turned over a soiled
collection, leaving in their wake
a nutrient enriched place.

They edged warily below me, feigning
indifference to my presence though I stood
transfixed, perched in thoughts, scratching
an anxiety that in these gardens my residency
would never turn over so many new leaves.

From Garden to Gallery

After a day at the George Brown Botanical Gardens, Darwin
and Ben Quilty's, 'After Afghanistan',
Museum & Art Gallery of the Northern Territory

In the Garden I cross the threshold of glasshouses
seeking succor with bromeliads
whose leaves are banded
with scales, like blotting paper, to inhale
this morning's fog:

outside I meander amongst upright
natives: one is shaped
like a pine but with large
glossy leaves and globular masses,
like pom-poms, of yellow and white flowers
brewed long ago, I am told on a sign, against
colds, vomiting and diarrhea; another stately elder
has large prop roots once weaved
into nets and dilly-bags, the strips
of bark chewed
into slings and tourniquets; while another
upholds a central cabbage, eaten raw
or lightly cooked, with the fronds
and flower bracts recycled
constructed containers:

in a cycad grove
I bear witness to ancient symbiosis –
coralloid root structures hosting
blue-green algae for nitrogen – and I read
how highly toxic seeds were once
de-husked and chipped into bite-size pieces

in a pounded baptism administering
coarse smelly flour:

before these gardens grew
asbestos was composted
in a cyclone's ruins
and I mull over a buried fibre's bloom:

the gardens and gallery are linked
by a Larrakia Dreamtime Walk
where dot-painted signs award
canoe trees, delicacies and the raw
stuffs for baskets and mats; and amidst signage
warning against camping and public drinking
our countrymen gather
a mountain of casks, prizefighting
and swilling their losses:

in the gallery I enter 'After Afghanistan',
another remote colonised community,
where trauma is scraped
and bandaged onto boards; where foot soldiers
are removed of their packaging
and left flailing, broken
and captured on a gallery's walls; and with eyes
clenched against the blinding expectation imposed
from inside I wait for the seepage
of blood from thighs – a self-mutilation
like the latex collected and heated from milkwood.

New Moon

For my bardibardi kujaka:
Gloria Friday, Marjorie Keighran & Clara Roberts

This is my recovery road, to follow the bardibardi
into the Gulf's wild pharmacy; I let myself
                surrender
    to those hallelujah hands outstretched
to a sandalwood's leafy collection
        dis one dumbuyumbu an millad mob
        boil jungkayi tea, tis pick you up:

        continuing to choose our leaves
between cabbage palms and billygoat plums, three kinds
    of paperbarks and bikabaji green plums,
we arrive at a shrub, dog's balls, and everyone
cracks it: *tis one kurranga, dem hangin' sweet lil-fruit:*

as we walk these medicine trails of baked black earth
      we watchfully step the tessellated tiles
          of the sandy-poor bush floor
and the bardibardi sing their appeasement to spirits –
      corralling us gently to a billabong's shade:

        we wash our leaves
before adding them to a billycan's brown rolling boil
      and as we drink together
the bardibardi tell me of the blind mermaid
              of Robinson River:

a moonstricken old lady
who journeyed to an exhaustion's
drowning in a billabong's calm lily pad
run on water:

her blind transformation from breathless
air to a reservoir's faint trailing
song percolates through this *lost city*
of stratified sandstone spires and columns
as the curlew cries against the acclaimed
phases of the moon:

depression scarring
is cheeky history breaching
the efficacy of our bardibardi's jungkayi bush brew –
and in a spent aftermath
we are left reading leaves for traces
of blind worry-bird's shared resurrection
in the slender crescent of a new moon.

The Stick

During my time of residency in Borroloola, 2011–2015, more than a dozen young adults passed away by suicide or violent death. Substance abuse is rife – especially of sugar, tobacco, ganja and alcohol – and too many young people have criminal convictions for petty violence and property misdemeanors. But the town has poor access to mental health care with specialist services usually provided in Katherine (700 kilometres, distance) or Darwin (960 kilometres). Borroloola is 'out of sight and out of mind': a place where immense community need is too often met with disengaged and inconsistent government service. Borroloola's health clinic, I am told by Indigenous family, is infamous for making Indigenous clients wait while non-Indigenous people are prioritized. Some openly racist administration workers in one government agency have their employment survive every complaint and protest. I have been slandered, more than once, for not knowing my place in non-Indigenous society. Borroloola is a town of shocking division where bigotry is just one more obstacle that First Australians must navigate.

In remote places like Borroloola, mental health care, especially for young adults, is in crisis. And what of education, the other main area of government service for young people? Throughout my time in Borroloola school attendance figures have stubbornly remained at around 57%. If conditions are so over-crowded and stressful at home why can't an air-conditioned comfortable school get kids to attend? The school works in partnership with a local mine to manage a Trust that facilitates vocational education, camps and sporting opportunities. Theoretically this Trust exits to compensate local First Australians for lost access to Country but, by the time the school and mine have enforced strict school attendance and behavior requirements for attending these 'opportunities', the school's ratio of

97% Indigenous is sometimes reversed in favour of non-Indigenous students. The school and mine are right to have high expectations for all students but what of reengagement programs and second chances? I was too often forced to comfort students because they had been excluded from vocational education or sporting camps. Teachers like me are too easily made to feel like we are working against a system that often appears uncompromising and slow to engage with the frustrations and challenges of Indigenous youth. The bardibardi, for example, continually ask for segregated upper primary and secondary classes; it is culturally so much more sensitive. And they would like their grandchildren educated in Language and Culture alongside Australian Curriculum.

In 2012, partly in response to these community aspirations, I established a First Australians storytelling group that met every Friday afternoon after school. Our club was called Diwurruwurru, which means 'message stick'. We proudly used this name with permission as we celebrated Indigenous Culture, Language and Aboriginal English and noisily partied with afternoon tea, story and poetry. We ran camps and Culture retreats, collaborated with The Australian Literacy and Numeracy Foundation to establish an annual poetry festival in Tennant Creek; published member poems electronically on *The Barkly Poetry Wall* and in the print publication *Coming to Voice*. In 2015 we published a book, with Blank Rune Press, showcasing the best of our work. In 2013 the club also collaborated with the Northern Territory Writers' Centre to secure an Australia Council grant to host Lionel Fogarty and Amanda King (a digital artist) in a month-long residency in Borroloola. This exciting program saw Borroloola school students writing poetry, learning to perform and then recording their efforts onto film. In 2014 twenty members from Diwurruwurru were invited to WordStorm, the Northern Territory Writers' Festival, to launch the Borroloola poetry film onto the national stage – a wonderful celebration of creativity in the Gulf.

At Diwurruwurru we developed a unique strategy for the creation of group poems. Our creative process was to meet around a meal or afternoon tea where we shared a lot of excited ideas and stories. I then gathered these together on a whiteboard where the drafting process began with much discussion, debate and hilarious attempts to pronounce and spell Aboriginal English and Language words. I do not standardize this spelling. Aboriginal English is a consequence of colonialism, of different language groups being forced to live together, but it is also a glorious linguistic invention that testifies, powerfully, to cultural resilience and pride. I hope to highlight this linguistic dynamism in the work of Diwurruwurru. So, after the initial attempts to capture a story onto a whiteboard, I would then work on the poem over the following week before bringing it back to the group for refinement and approval. This process was often repeated over several weeks. Diwurruwurru was always a lively creative place where family and friends would meet to explore, experiment and assert First Australians' Culture and Story. The message stick that it generously shared was one of pride, respect and strength.

Following is one of our group poems, called 'Da Barri Barri Bullet Train', about a Culture camp I organized with local First Australian leaders. It expresses beautifully the kids' pride in Culture and their intuitive longing for a commitment to 'two-ways learning':

we bin get up with mista an habim gooda one feed
we bin jumpin da mudika
an millad bin go lunga bush
mimi an kukudi bin come too
an dey bin singim kujika
dey bin learnim us mob
for sing im kujika
we likim learn for sing us mob kujika
wen us mob bin lyin down in da darkes
darkest night I bin look da barri barri
e bin movin really really like da bullet train
I bin hold ma mimi really tight
da fire us mob bin make next ta millad mob
poking tongue like a big one king brown
an millad mob listen noise one side na water
must e bin da buffalo drinkin water
den us bin listen da croc bin snap da buffalo

da ngabaya out there too
an he bin make us mob so frightn
but ma mimi bin sing out
hey you mob stop all da noise
ma mimi bin start to sing
da song na us mob country
sing in da old language
dem old people did sing
an make millad mob so shiny an strong
an I bin lyin da listen na mimi
I bin feel really really safe
den I musta bin go sleep

This poem so beautifully captures the comfort and security that First Australian kids receive in family and Culture. But prioritizing this in schools through a commitment to 'two-ways learning' is no longer deemed valuable. So, while the First Australian community is not empowered to express its aspirations for what a school might look like, ever more government data is collected. In education this has resulted in even further instability. The National Assessment Program – Literacy and Numeracy (NAPLAN) collects results that highlight Northern Territory disadvantages and challenges where 40–60% of Indigenous students are achieving below minimum standards in reading and writing. Consequently, bilingual education through 'two-way learning' is abolished in the hope that this will improve literacy results by concentrating on Standard English. And schools implement a growing list of literacy and numeracy programs looking for improvements in the statistics collected: QuickSmart Literacy and Numeracy; National Accelerated Literacy Programs; First Steps Literacy and Numeracy; Walking Talking Texts (for teaching English-as-an-additional-language); MultiLit (to address the needs of students with disabilities); Visible Learning; and now from 2015 Direct Instruction. And yet we know that nutrition and health are closely related to educational achievement, school attendance and literacy. The health status of remote First Australians is poor: more babies suffer low to extremely low birth-weight and upwards to 70%

of children suffer from chronic Otitis Media, a serious middle ear disease that can cause permanent hearing loss and inhibit language development. There are few figures on how widespread fetal alcohol spectrum disorder might be but anecdotally, First Australians in Borroloola believe that this sadness is so prevalent, the government might consider itself unable to afford a remedy; it is cheaper not to diagnose. So the focus remains on collecting approved data rather than supporting the 'whole child' and to listening to what the First Australian community wants.

This is why the Federal Government's Intervention into the lives of Northern Territory First Australians should be so shocking to us all: it is a bipartisan policy of disempowering our First Nations; of not trusting their voice; of failing to respect Culture; and ultimately, ironically, of not believing in the children whom Country truly sings. As my Borroloola students so generously shared with me in another group poem from Diwurruwurru called 'dance strong, dat country move en you':

> millad mob drive out bush long way
> over dem hills to make bend like dis
> an us mob see fresh tracks of big fulla
> big an black an he biggest mob angry
> he angry like wounded beast
> with horns so wild an he growl us
> but dis country ours an millad mob
> know it good way so us drive on
> all way to wandangnula
> dem whitefullas call police lagoon
> but us mob know it right way
> an us see dem hills so biggest dry
> an know where dat wurnamburna is
> you know mista dat white ochre
> it bend down like dis
> an it hard but there biggest pack
> ochre to mix with water an dig
> millad mob dig like dis an fill
> dem buckets right way dat white ochre

for dance an make us dance strong like tru
aboriginal an make dat country move en you
us mob paint dat ochre here
on the face like dis an on our arms here
sum mob paint it on dem chest here an on legs
here an here but not us mob
millad mob paint here an here an here
like dis you see do it good way
an den us line up an start to move swingin
our arms an stompin feet to kick dust
it dance for country swingin stompin
lit by ochre as dem singers breathe
da language only dem old people know
us mob just too deadly steppin singin

                                    up dat storm.

This group poem is such a vibrant expression of pride in family
and Cultural identity. The way the kids incorporate non-verbal com-
munication into everyday speech, the interrogation of colonial values
and the assertion of First Australian rights is remarkable. It is a breach
of trust to lose faith in these 'deadly' kids as they 'sing up their storm'.
I have met so many passionate and good people working in remote
services, whether that be in education, health or justice, but there must
be more accountability, and First Australians must be listened to. You
cannot work successfully if you do not first sit down and listen.

In the Gulf of Carpentaria it is more than just good manners
to sit down with people and to listen and seek permission before
beginning work. There is no single 'senior law man' who can speak
for community or give permission for the telling of stories or to enter
homelands. This is most commonly a non-Indigenous stereotype
of how remote First Australian communities function. In the Gulf
every person is the Traditional Owner, or 'boss', of a particular part
of country. Every person, male and female, is both *ngimarringki* (or
'owner') for their father's country and *jungkayi* (or 'manager') of their
mother's country. The former have primary spiritual responsibility for

protecting the estate, including sacred sites, and the latter organise ceremonies and decide whether outsiders may enter the estate (they also have responsibility for the songlines connected with their estate). Community engagement requires 'slow time', and permission to begin work and to experience and share culture must be sought from as many people as possible.

The kids of Borroloola have so much pride in the colour of their skin and in Culture. They want to be listened to and they love to share stories concerning Culture and what life is like 'out bush'. They also demand to be respected as individuals and to have the specific rights and responsibilities of their clan respected. They are Aboriginal people of the Yanyuwa, Marra, Gudanji or Garrwa Language groups. And they are as different from one another as French people are from Germans. The kids of Diwurruwurru reminded me of this, in a sequence of group poems called 'Gemstones for Mista', two of which read as follows:

Yanyuwa and Garrwa Gem

us father country wid baribari
out Dommadgee way an dem
baribari crash down da ground
an leave Dreaming only us mob do know
but us mother country is brolga one
an millad mob Traditional Owner of dat one
dey men business an very important
dem brolga eat da grasses an grasshoppers
an sing a squawkin funny song
us all dance dat way an sing
da sun away but wait
you remember dem men
who die well all dem men are brolga
who dance all thru da day
dem brolga da Traditional Owner
of Borroloola an make millad mob
remember great great grandfather

dat how us mob know
dis country all our country
it all millad mob country
we sing an speak for it
us mob all tru god

*

Gudanji Gem

millad mob not saltwater mob
like dem yanyuwa mob
us gudanji mob, dis millad country
an you come drive in mudika long way
out bush an us show you dis lagoon
it long long way you know
dat devil devil dreaming
you don't climb him or dance
da night dat ngabaya bin stay
an he chock you like tis
you drive long long way past him
past barramundi dreaming swallowed
in mine an you see high on ridge
where freshwater kangaroo bash
dat saltwater one dat where millad country is
us mob sing dat place wid ceremony
an lagoon big country full
taddle, long-nose, fish an bush turkey
water lily, makulu, bush plum, onion an yam
you bend roun' unda massacre hill like dis
– dem cheeky whitefullas call him dat –
an up a track past dat skull creek
in da cave a baby blackfulla bone
tis sung to stone like crystal memory

*

These kids know that they speak for Country; they know exactly who is boss for what and who is charged with which Songlines and Ceremonies. They have within them an astounding knowledge and orientation of Country, and can trace back through numerous generations how one person is related to another – relationship with Country and family is everything. Most Borroloola kids do not have access to Language, but the Language words that describe family relationships and connection to Country (often through bush tucker and medicine), remain strong in their Aboriginal English. They also know where the sites connected with massacre are located, where the bones are collected and remembered, and how no payback has been allowed. Now mining also disturbs sickness sites, and gouges through the sacred sites connected with rainbow serpents, making people who are charged with their care sick. But despite all this cheeky and rough mistreatment, this shocking contact history, the people stand defiant and strong. They share so generously with anyone willing to sit still and listen. And, with me, the people of Borroloola shared more than story and history.

After I was adopted into Gudanji life I took on new privileges and responsibilities. I enjoyed greater access to Culture and family but also had more duty to share. One consequence of this was that Ty and Trishanne became my lil-brother and sister and lived with my partner and me, on-and-off, so that they could enjoy the friendships to be found in town rather than the quiet and isolation of living out bush. Sitting around a fire in the backyard they shared so much pride in Culture. Trishanne is a wonderfully engaging person, so cleverly comic and assertive and is a leading member of Diwurruwurru, so she really enjoyed the additional time we had to craft poems together and celebrate the strength of the Gudanji. She grieved for the damage done to Country by mining (and for the sickness it caused to Nana Miller). So in one poem Trishanne announced:

Millad Green Diamond

This is millad mob memory of place.
I been looking for it long time,
all day I search (you ask anyone).
I wait and see (and guess what)
I find it just like I knew.
I keep this diamond safe and strong.
It the stone from us mob Country
and it has secret name in language.
So secret in the Song from millad mob land.
It come to us before the mine.
Millad mob sing that place strong and good,
but now that mine hurt our Country.
It turns birds so red
with iron dust they can not fly,
trees so red they can not breathe
the good air or feel the bright sun.
Why can't this mine see that this stone
is so precious,
see that us Aboriginal people always care,
always speak for this land.

This poem powerfully responds to the damage done to Country by mining. To the way in which First Australians not only lose access to Country but also to the connected parts of Ceremony and Law – it disrupts Songlines and disturbs 'sickness sites'. Mining companies collude with governments to deny First Australians royalty payments, and the legal right to oppose mining, by extinguishing native title in leases. It is a cynical abuse of native title law.

Trishanne and Ty were there when Nana Miller sung me as jungkayi for Jayipa. They stood in the same relationship to this special place, a permanent lagoon rich in resources and at the intersection of many Dreaming Trails. Knowing my pride in this connection to Country they shared many stories with me about this place, history that had been taught to them by Nana Miller, like the incident interrogated above in 'Millad Green Diamond'. Many of these stories involved interactions with spirits and magic and were always a potent challenge to my secular humanism. In another poem Trishanne celebrated a time we spent camping at Jayipa. This is another poem that defiantly raises the flag of pride, powerfully delighting in familial relationships and in those intimate connections to Country:

Old Pride

I go fishing at Jayipa
With my family sitting in sand
When we hear these three old men walking
Out of the west and speaking
Their Gudanji soul smeared
In golden ochre, carrying spears
And wearing djulu for pride.

This makes us all so
Brolga joyful, leaping and trumpeting
To the world this welcome
To Culture and Country –
This strong one memory of place.

We hear the shimmering fat
Fish in the billabong lined
With waterlily, yam and bush onion –
Our feast in place.
It is getting dark so we pack
Our daylight, knowing our love
And strength for caring
And speaking for this place.

We travel to the Dreaming Rock
To celebrate the croc and the frog
And how the old man croc won't share
The water so the poor parched frog is forced

To step and dodge his way
To life.

We take photos to add to our memories
As we speak for this place. We call
Out our hunger searching
For a killer
To feast our family. This Country
Will always look after us
As we cook our feed
In a grand ground oven.

Later at night
As we trace satellites ducking
In and out of those stars
We lay in our swags rolling from side to side
Beneath the Dreaming Hill surrounded
By love and pride in our special place.

I am so joyous for the part I have been allowed to play in facilitating such poetry of defiance and praise. Such expression takes 'slow time' but literacy need not be an obstacle to this compelling and irreplaceable poetry. Diwurruwurru is a feast that I wished more Australians shared.

Glossary

Arwuju: is Gudanji for nana or grandmother, on your father's side.

Baba: is Gudanji for siblings, a less formal term of address.

Bardibardi: is Yanyuwa for respectfully referring to older women.

Baribari: originally a Yanyuwa word meaning 'that dangerous star, the shooting star'. It was believed that these phenomena could make you sick, even make you die. Baribari has now entered Kriol and is used commonly by all the Gulf's Indigenous people when referring to shooting stars. There remains a belief that this phenomenon can be dangerous, so when camping out bush you are advised not to sleep on your back, with your mouth open, because a shooting star might steal your spirit.

Bunyi: is Kriol in the Gulf region of northern Australia for backside.

Buja: is Kriol in the Gulf region of northern Australia for brother.

Diwurruwurru: is Yanyuwa/Garrwa for 'message stick'.

Djulu: is Indigenous language in the Gulf of Carpentaria for the loincloth traditionally worn by men.

Gangu: is Gudanji for pop or grandfather, on your father's side.

Gargalingu: is Gudanji for sister, a more formal term of address.

Gargalu: is Gudanji for brother, a more formal term of address.

Garrwa: one of four surviving Indigenous language groups in the Northern Territory's Gulf of Carpentaria.

Gudanji: one of four surviving Indigenous language groups in the Northern Territory's Gulf of Carpentaria.

Jigga:	is Kriol in the Gulf region of northern Australia for brother.
Julayarriyarri:	is Yanyuwa for the northern Australian meteorological phenomenon known in English as Morning Glory Cloud.
Jungkayi:	is Yanyuwa/Garrwa for a person who stands in a guardian relationship to the ceremonies of managing his/her mother's Country. Today this term is often used to mean 'boss', 'most important' or even 'policeman' and is also used widely by members of the Gudanji and Mara people.
Kardu:	is Garrwa for uncle.
Kujaka:	is Yanyuwa/Garrwa for respectfully referring to your mother and her sisters.
Kujika:	is Yanyuwa for Songlines; Indigenous Country 'beats with the rhythm of Kujika'.
Kukudi:	is Garrwa for nana or grandmother, on your mother's side.
Long Nose:	is colloquial in the Gulf region of northern Australia for freshwater crocodile.
Malbu:	is Yanyuwa for respectfully referring to older men.
Marra:	one of four surviving Indigenous language groups in the Northern Territory's Gulf of Carpentaria.
Millad:	is Kriol in the Gulf region of northern Australia for the first person plural pronoun: we, us, our.
Mimi:	is Yanyuwa for pop or grandfather, on your mother's side.
Mudika:	is Kriol in the Gulf region of northern Australia for motorcar.
Mugkbali:	is Gudanji for family.
Munanga:	originally a Yanyuwa word meaning 'stranger, the one not known to me, white person' but has now entered Kriol and is used commonly by all the Gulf's Indigenous people when referring, often derisively, to 'whitefullas'.

Munga-munga: is Indigenous language in the Gulf region of northern Australia for girl or young woman; perhaps originally a Yanyuwa word, this term is now used widely by most Indigenous people of the Gulf.

Ngabaya: is Indigenous language in the Gulf region of northern Australia for ghost or spirit; perhaps originally a Yanyuwa word, this term is now used widely by most Indigenous people of the Gulf.

Nuwalinya: is Indigenous language in the Gulf region of northern Australia for mermaid; perhaps originally a Yanyuwa word, this term is now used widely by most Indigenous people of the Gulf.

Taddle: is Kriol in the Gulf region of northern Australia for turtle.

Twobula: is Kriol in the Gulf region of northern Australia for two.

Yalinga: is Yanyuwa/Garrwa for foreskin. This word should not be voiced out loud as it is connected with Ceremony. It should be read as foreskin during public readings. It is often used in the Gulf, usually by young males, to cause offence.

Yanyuwa: one of four surviving Indigenous language groups in the Northern Territory's Gulf of Carpentaria.

'Turtle Camp' quotes the following lines of Yanyuwa:

bawuji barra...
wingkayarra wingkayarra kayikaji ka-wingkala barra...
yuwu wakara nyinku na-alanji wurrbi...

They can be translated as:

You have finished now...
Go, go, go quickly now...
Yes, you have found it – your true home...

(Thanks to John Bradley, *Singing Saltwater Country: Journey to the Songlines of Carpentaria*, Allen & Unwin, 2010).

Acknowledgements

I am enriched by the love of a large family, and I am bound to them all, but I especially treasure my parents, Ray and Joan, my partner, Jillian, & my four children: Rhiannon (and Jason Bardsley), Aidan (and Jessica Esveld), Ceinwen and Kian – you pick up my pieces making me whole.

The poetry in this volume has been greatly supported by the editorial advice and encouragement of: Margaret Bradstock, Anne Elvey, Ceinwen Hall, Kian Hall, Rhiannon Hall, Tim Heffernan, Judith Rodriguez, Melinda Smith & Terri-ann White. As always, my first confidant and editor is Jillian Hall. I could do nothing without her generosity and expertise (my lover with a first class honours degree in Early English Literature and Language from the University of Sydney).

I am dumbfounded (and so relieved) that UWAP has given me a guernsey. I would like to especially thank: Nicole Van Kan, Colin Barr, Connie Sze, Kate Pickard, Charlotte Guest, and of course, the indomitable Terri-ann White. I hope I kick straight.

My grateful acknowledgment to the following e-journals and their editors: *Cordite Poetry Review* (edited by Cassandra Atherton, Pam Brown, Penelope Goodes, Carol Jenkins, Matthew Hall, Paul Hetherington, Kent MacCarter, Tracy Ryan, Omar Sakr and Fiona Wright); *Meniscus* (edited by Dallas John Baker, Paul Hetherington, Shane Strange and Jen Webb); *Plumwood Mountain: An Australian Journal of Ecopoetry & Ecopoetics* (edited by Stuart Cooke, Tricia Dearborn, Anne Elvey and Peter Minter); *Tincture* (edited by Stuart Barnes & Daniel Young) and *Verity La* (edited by Stuart Barnes, Alise Blayney, Tim Heffernan & Michelle Seminara); and the print publications: *Best Australian Poems 2015* (Black Inc Publishing, edited by Geoff Page); *Best Australian Poems 2016* (Black Inc Publishing, edited by Sarah Holland-Batt); *Best Australian Poems 2017* (Black Inc Publishing, edited by Sarah Holland-Batt); *Contemporary Australian Poetry* (Puncher & Wattmann, edited by Judith Beveridge, Judy Johnson, Martin Langford & David Musgrave); *Meanjin* (edited by Judith Beveridge)*; Offshoots: Contemporary Life Writing Methodologies & Practice in Australia* (edited by Donna Brien and Quinn Eades); *Rabbit Poetry Journal* (edited by Sally Evans, Alison Whittaker and Jessica Wilkinson); *Southerly* (edited by David Brooks, Andy Jackson and Kate Lilley) and *Westerly* (edited by Lucy Dougan, Steve Kinnane and Catherine Noske), where many of these poems first appeared.

Much earlier versions of the following poems appear in my book, *Sweetened in Coals:* 'Borroloola Class', 'Carpentaria Running the Flag', 'Concourse' and 'Dystopian Empire'. 'Borroloola Blue' is also included in that publication.

A selection of poems from *Fume* were published in the chapbook, *Borroloola Class,* by IPSI (International Poetry Studies Institute) which is part of the Centre for Creative and Cultural Research at the University of Canberra. I am very thankful to Owen Bullock, Paul Munden and Shane Strange for their encouragement and editorial advice.

I am grateful to the University of Wollongong's creative arts faculty, where I received so much encouragement and direction while studying for a Doctor of Creative Arts; and I would like to especially thank Alan Wearne and Pete Minter.

I am greatly indebted to John Bradley, *Singing Saltwater Country: Journey to the Songlines of Carpentaria* (Allen & Unwin, 2010), Shellie Morris & The Borroloola Song Women, *Together We Are Strong: Ngambala Wiji Li-Wunungu* (ABC and Universal Music, 2013), Tony Roberts, *Frontier Justice: A History of the Gulf Country to 1900* (University of Queensland Press, 2005), Alexis Wright,

Grog War (Magabala Books, Broome, 1997, 2009) and Gulf Country Musecology Project for Waralungku Arts, *Gulf Country Songbook: Yanyuwa, Marra, Garrwa and Gudanji Songs* (2015).

'Professional Conduct': after Jan Senbergs, 'Otway Night', 1994, Synthetic polymer paint on canvas, AGNSW: http://www.artgallery.nsw.gov.au/collection/works/594.1994/

All of the poetry in *Fume* was written in Borroloola between 2011 and 2015, but much of this writing was reworked and first read publicly while I enjoyed a residency at the Eco House, The George Brown Botanic Gardens in Darwin. I am very grateful to the Northern Territory Writers' Centre for giving me this wonderful opportunity.